The Sermon on the Mount

and other Bible Stories

Retold by Vic Parker

Miles Kelly

First published in 2011 by Miles Kelly Publishing Ltd
Harding's Barn, Bardfield End Green, Thaxted, Essex, CM6 3PX, UK

This edition printed in 2011

2 4 6 8 10 9 7 5 3

EDITORIAL DIRECTOR *Belinda Gallagher*
ART DIRECTOR *Jo Cowan*
EDITOR *Carly Blake*
DESIGNERS *Michelle Cannatella, Joe Jones*
JUNIOR DESIGNER *Kayleigh Allen*
COVER DESIGNER *Joe Jones*
CONSULTANT *Janet Dyson*
PRODUCTION MANAGER *Elizabeth Collins*
REPROGRAPHICS *Stephan Davis, Ian Paulyn*

ISBN 978-1-84810-400-6

Printed in China

British Library Cataloguing-in-Publication Data
A catalogue record for this book is available from the British Library

ACKNOWLEDGEMENTS
The publishers would like to thank the following artists
who have contributed to this book:

The Bright Agency Katriona Chapman, Dan Crisp,
Giuliano Ferri, Mélanie Florian (inc. cover)
Advocate Art Andy Catling, Alida Massari

*The publishers would like to thank Robert Willoughby and
the London School of Theology for their help in compiling this book.*

Made with paper from a sustainable forest

www.mileskelly.net   info@mileskelly.net

www.factsforprojects.com
Self-publish your
children's book

buddingpress.co.uk

Contents

Wonders at Capernaum

Worshippers in synagogues who heard Jesus preach were always amazed at the way He spoke. Jesus didn't just read out the ancient holy writings as most Jewish teachers did, He actually explained them.

One day, Jesus was in the synagogue at Capernaum, in the middle of giving a

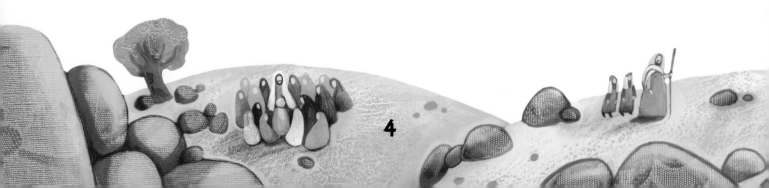

speech, when a man burst out of the crowd around Him and started shouting wildly. "I know who you are!" he yelled, pointing his finger threateningly in Jesus' face. "You're a messenger from God. And I know what you've been sent to do, you have come to destroy us all!"

As the crowd gasped in shock, Jesus remained calm. "Be quiet," He commanded. Then He shut his eyes and after a moment said sternly, "Leave him alone!"

All at once the man fainted and crumpled to the floor. When he recovered, he seemed to be a completely different person. He was quiet and calm, if somewhat confused. There had been demons inside the man, but Jesus had ordered them out.

All those who witnessed this incredible event couldn't believe their eyes and ears. Who is this Jesus of Nazareth they wondered? What sort of strange powers does He have that He is able to command demons?

Meanwhile, Jesus had gone to Peter's house. Peter told Him that his mother-in-law was very ill with an extremely high temperature and begged Jesus to visit her to see if He could help. Jesus stood by the bedside of the sick woman who was shivering and sweating with fever, and groaning in pain. Jesus took her hand and said simply but firmly, "Be well." Straight away the hot flush seemed to fade from her cheeks. She stopped writhing around and her breathing calmed. Then she

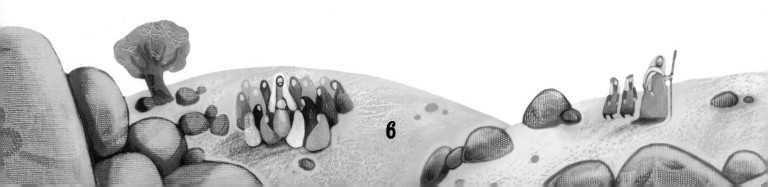

opened her eyes, looked around at everyone and said, "What am I doing in bed? Peter, you should have told me we had guests. Now what would everyone like to eat and drink?" And she got up and began bustling around.

News of what happened at the synagogue and at Peter's house spread around Capernaum and the surrounding towns in no time. Before sunset, there was a long queue outside Peter's door, everyone wanting to see Jesus. People had come from miles around, begging to be cured of all sorts of illnesses. They had brought their sick relations and friends with them too.

Very patiently, Jesus saw them all, one by one. Before the night had ended, He had placed his hands upon every single person and they had all been cured.

Jesus left Capernaum early next morning, so as not to cause a fuss. But as soon as the grateful townspeople realized he had gone, they tracked Him down and begged Him to

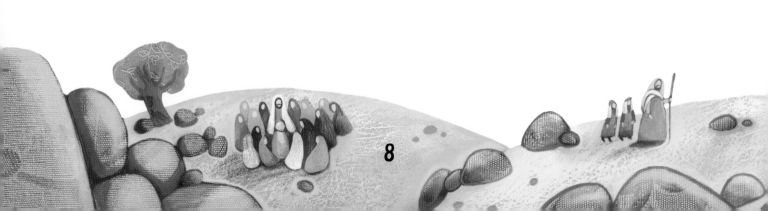

stay. "I'm afraid I can't," Jesus insisted. "People in other places need me. I have to tell everyone how they can find happiness by turning to God. It is what I have been sent to do." And He and His followers, called disciples, went on their way.

Matthew chapters 7, 8; Luke chapter 4

Jesus the Healer

Soon people from far and wide came to hear about Jesus. Men, women and children were excited by the sound of this captivating preacher who worked miracles. They began seeking Jesus out, travelling to wherever He was to see Him for themselves. Jesus tried to help as many people as He could and convince them to turn to God.

After Jesus had preached in one place, a man who was suffering from the terrible skin disease leprosy crept up to Him. He was extremely nervous about approaching Jesus. Leprosy was very contagious and also incurable, and most people didn't want lepers anywhere near them. In fact, people usually ran away when they saw a leper coming. But Jesus didn't. The poor man knelt before Him, his skin misshapen and ugly with sores, and said, "I know that you can cure me, if you want to."

"Of course I want to," Jesus murmured, and He reached out and placed His hand on the leper's crumbling skin.

It took a couple of moments for the leper to recover from the shock. After all, most people wouldn't dream of touching him.

But then the man looked at his hands, his legs and felt his face. His skin was healed. He was cured!

"Don't tell anyone," Jesus told the man, who was sobbing his gratitude. "Just go to your priest so he can see for himself and make an offering of thanks to God."

Another time, Jesus shocked many people when He helped an officer in the Roman army. After all, most Jewish people hated the Romans because they had taken control of Israel. The Roman officer begged Jesus to help his servant who was lying ill at home in great

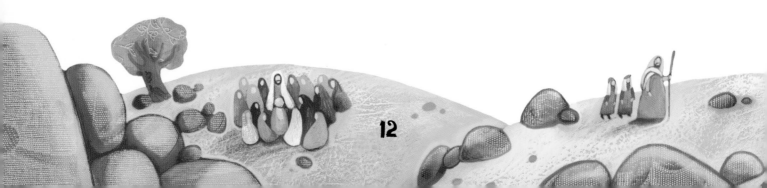

pain. "I will come with you straight away," Jesus told the Roman officer.

"That won't be necessary," the Roman insisted. "I know if you just give the word for my servant to recover, he will do so."

Jesus was stunned and delighted. "I haven't met a Jewish person who has shown as much faith as this," He said. "There will be many people from far-off lands who will be able to enter the Kingdom of Heaven, while many from the nation of Israel will be locked outside."

The Roman officer returned home to find his servant completely cured.

Matthew chapter 8; Mark chapter 1; Luke chapter 7; John chapter 4

Jesus Forgives Sins

One day Jesus was preaching in a house in Capernaum that was full of people. Many of them were important Jewish people such as officials, priests and Pharisees. These highly regarded elders had travelled from all over Israel to see for themselves the preacher everyone was talking about. They had many questions they wanted answering. Who was Jesus? Was He a trickster, or a prophet like Elijah? Was He really the Messiah spoken of in the ancient holy books? And what was Jesus teaching? They didn't want Jesus leading everyone astray. After all He wasn't even a priest with training in Jewish holy laws.

There were so many people in the house. They were jammed shoulder-to-shoulder in each room and wedged into the hall, spilling out into the street. Outside there were many more, straining to hear and get a glimpse of Jesus through the windows.

While Jesus spoke, four latecomers staggered up to the house carrying a paralyzed friend on a stretcher. They were determined to get close enough to ask Jesus to heal their companion. When they saw

there was no
chance of
getting in the
front door, they
came up with a
plan. They
climbed up the
outside stairs and
onto the roof. Then
they tied ropes onto
the stretcher, removed
some of the roof covering, and
slowly and carefully lowered their friend
through the gap, right in front of Jesus.

Jesus was moved by the lengths the men
had gone to. He realized they must have
huge faith in Him and great love for their
sick friend. He looked down at the suffering

man, placed His hand on his head and said, "Take heart, your sins are forgiven."

At His words the room erupted into uproar. The Jewish officials and holy men were outraged. They could believe that Jesus might perhaps have genuine powers of healing, but no one had the power to forgive sins except God Himself. Jesus was committing a terrible sin by saying He could do so. In fact, under Jewish law it was the crime of blasphemy for which He could be severely punished.

Jesus signalled for everyone to calm down and the room gradually fell silent. He asked, "Do you think it's easier for me to say, 'I forgive your sins,' or for me to say, 'Get up off that stretcher, you can now walk'?" The Jewish elders mumbled to each other. Of course it was easier for Jesus to say that He had done something which they couldn't see. Jesus went on, "Maybe you'll believe that God has given me the power to heal this man's soul if I heal his body too."

Jesus looked into the eyes of the man lying stiff and still on his stretcher. "My friend, get up and walk," He said.

To everyone's amazement, he did. The Jewish officials and holy men left the house with more new questions than answers.

Matthew chapter 9; Mark chapter 2; Luke chapter 5

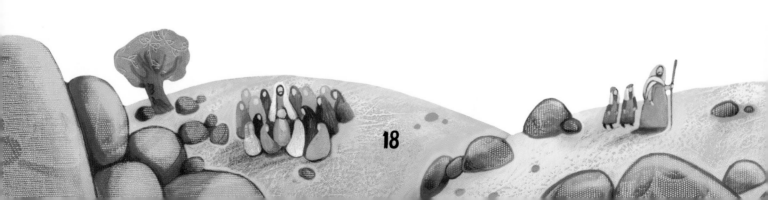

Jesus Chooses Special Helpers

Jesus became so well known that He couldn't go anywhere without being surrounded by crowds. He once climbed high up a mountain so He could be on His own. Jesus prayed to God all night. When He came down the next day, He summoned twelve men from His many disciples.

They were brothers Peter and Andrew,

brothers James and John, a former follower of John the Baptist called Philip, Matthew the tax collector, a man called Simon who was a member of a Jewish group called the Zealots, a second James, and four others – Thomas, Bartholomew, Thaddaeus and Judas Iscariot.

Jesus took the twelve men to one side and spoke to them. "I want you to be my special helpers," He explained. "I want each of you to go and preach to people what I have preached. I am going to give you the power to heal the sick, just as I do. Don't accept any money for it. Don't take anything on your travels except for the clothes you are wearing, just live off people's kindness. It won't be easy – some people will ignore you, others will try to stop you spreading my message and some may even try to have you killed. But God will always be with you, looking after you, and His Holy Spirit will give you courage. And if you give up your life for me, I promise you will have a new and happier life in Heaven."

So for several weeks, the twelve men went out around the countryside, teaching and healing in Jesus' name.

Matthew chapter 10; Mark chapters 3, 6; Luke chapters 6, 9

The Sermon on the Mount

One day a vast crowd gathered to hear Jesus speak, so He went up a hillside so that everyone could see and hear Him.

"Blessed are all those who realize that God is missing from their lives," He preached, "for they will one day enter Heaven. Blessed are all sad people, for they will be comforted. Blessed are gentle people, for all the Earth will be theirs. Blessed are those who try to live good lives, for they will be well rewarded. Blessed are those who take pity on others, for they will be shown pity too. Blessed are those with pure hearts, for they will see God. Blessed are those who work for peace, for God cares for them as His own children. Blessed are those who follow God but are made to suffer because of it – the Kingdom of Heaven will belong to them. I want you all to follow my teachings even if people make it difficult for you. I want you to be like a light, showing others the right way."

Everyone was quiet and listening so hard, you could almost hear the plants growing.

"Don't think that I am telling you to forget about the old religious teachings and rules," Jesus went on. "I'm telling you to pay more attention to them than ever. You've been told that it is a sin to kill anyone. I'm telling you that you should not even argue with anyone. You've been told that you should not take something that belongs to someone else just because you want it. I'm telling you that you shouldn't even think about it in the first place. You've been told that if someone is nasty to you, it's alright to get your own back. I'm telling you that you should forget it and do nothing.

"You should treat your enemies the same as you treat your friends. And don't hoard riches and luxuries on Earth where they can be stolen or destroyed. Instead think of good deeds as coins, and try to stack them

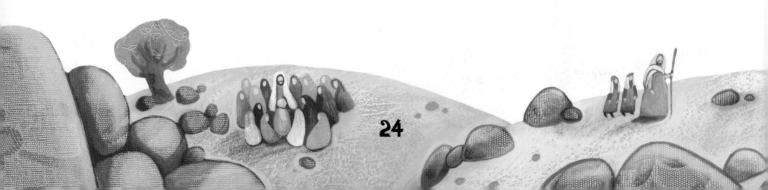

up. But don't boast – God knows everything anyway. Lastly, don't worry about everyday things such as how you are going to pay for food to eat or clothes to wear. If you put your energy into looking for God, He will look after you in turn."

Then Jesus told everyone how to pray. "Go somewhere quiet where you can be alone," He said, "and talk to God directly, as if you were talking to a friend. Just say whatever is in your heart. If there is anything you need, ask Him for it and He will give it to you." And he taught them a special prayer beginning with the words 'Our Father'.

Jesus gave a sad smile. "If you do as I say, you will be like a wise man who builds his home on rock and it will stand firm. But if you take no notice, you will be like a fool who builds his home on sand. The wind will blow it down and the rain will wash it away, until the house is in ruins."

Matthew chapters 5 to 7; Luke chapters 6, 11

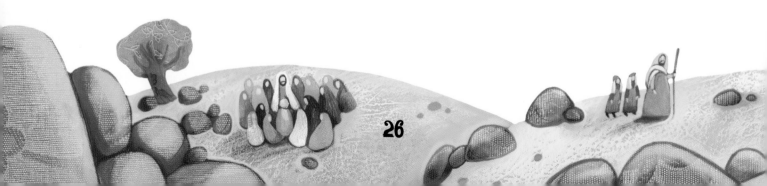

The Miracle at the Pool

Jesus once went to Jerusalem to attend an important religious festival. While he was there, he visited a holy pool at a place called Bethesda. The pool was always surrounded by many sick and injured people. They gathered there hoping to bathe in the water and be miraculously cured. It was believed that every so often an angel stirred up the waters and the first person to bathe in the pool when this happened would be healed.

Jesus saw one man there who had been crippled for thirty-eight years. Jesus knew that he had been waiting by the pool for a very long time. Whenever the man saw ripples appear on the water, he would struggle to drag himself towards the edge of the pool. But moving was so slow and painful for him that other people always beat him to it. Even on the rare occasion that he made it

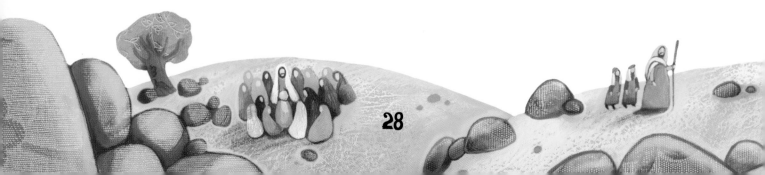

to the pool first, there was no one to help him get into the water.

Jesus felt great pity for the poor man and greatly admired him for his faith and courage. He decided that the man had waited long enough for a miracle. "Stand up and pick up your mat. You can walk," Jesus said.

And to the man's astonishment and joy, he did so. He went straight to the great temple to give thanks to God, taking delight in each step he took. A group of Jewish leaders were there and recognized him. "But you were crippled!" they marvelled. "Whatever has happened to you?"

"Jesus of Nazareth cured me," the man told them, and explained everything that had happened.

Instead of being pleased, the Jewish leaders were furious. Jesus had worked yet another miracle on the holy day of rest, the Sabbath. Outraged, they grew more determined than ever to get rid of Him.

John chapter 5

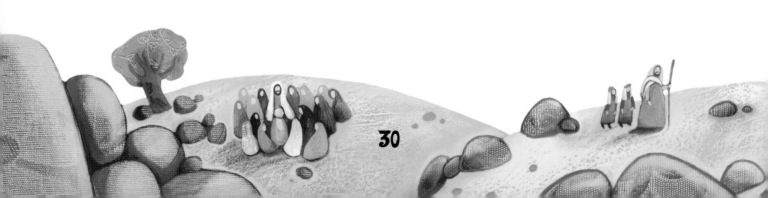

Two Fish and Five Loaves

There came a time when the King of Judea had John the Baptist, Jesus' good friend, thrown into prison and put to death. When Jesus heard the news, He was preaching at the Sea of Galilee. He was upset and wanted to escape the crowds who followed Him everywhere so He could be on His own for a little while. Jesus and His twelve disciples took a little boat out across the waters. However, the hundreds of people who had come to see and hear Jesus raced around the coast, joined by more people they met on the way. The crowd was there waiting for Jesus and His friends when they arrived on the far shore.

Jesus looked at the great mass of people – many of them sick or injured, hoping desperately for a cure. His heart went out to them. "Look at them," Jesus murmured. "They are like sheep without a shepherd."

Even though Jesus was grief-stricken and exhausted, He began preaching and healing… and was still talking to the people when dusk began to fall.

"Master, you've done enough now," the disciples said, concerned for Jesus. "It's time

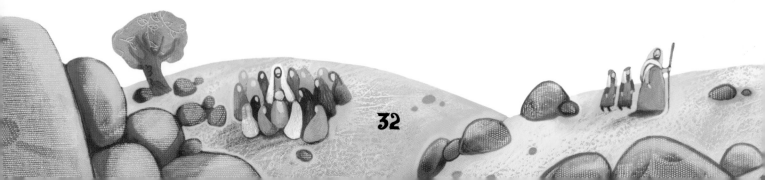

everyone went home. We all need something to eat."

Jesus smiled wearily. "No one needs to go anywhere," He said. "You can find us all some dinner."

The disciples looked at each other in confusion. They were surrounded by at least five thousand people. How did Jesus expect the disciples to feed them all?

"We've hardly any money between all of us to buy anything for supper," Philip pointed out.

Andrew added, "The only food we have is what this lad has brought with him," and he indicated a young boy carrying a basket. "He's got five loaves of bread and two fish, but they'll hardly go very far!"

Jesus stretched out his hands over the

loaves and fish, said a blessing and broke them into pieces. Then He told His disciples, "Now share them out among everyone."

The disciples knew that they should trust Jesus, no matter what. To their amazement, there was enough bread and fish for everybody to have a hearty supper and enough left over to fill twelve baskets.

Matthew chapter 14; Mark chapter 6; Luke chapter 9; John chapter 6

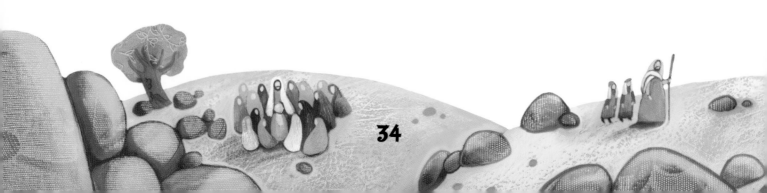

The Good Samaritan

Jesus always surprised people by knowing Jewish religious rules inside out and back to front. Many religious leaders and holy men who had spent their whole lives studying the laws were jealous of Jesus' knowledge. So they would ask tricky questions to try to catch Him out.

One day a lawyer came to Jesus and

asked, "What must I do to win eternal life?"

"What does the law tell you to do?" Jesus answered simply.

"To love God with all my heart and soul, and to love my neighbour as I love myself," the lawyer reeled off smugly, showing off his knowledge.

"Exactly," said Jesus. "If you already know, why are you asking me?"

"Ah, but who is my neighbour?" the man asked, feeling confident that he had posed a question far too difficult for Jesus to answer.

"Let me tell you a story," Jesus said, without a moment's hesitation. "There was once a man travelling on the road from Jerusalem to Jericho. Suddenly a group of bandits sprang out from behind some rocks

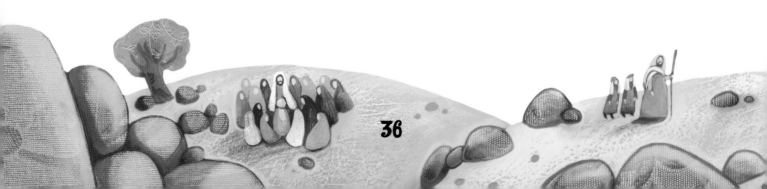

and attacked him. There was no one around to hear the traveller's cries for help. The bandits beat him, robbed him of all his possessions and left him for dead.

"After a while, a priest came walking down the road," Jesus continued. "He wondered what a bundle of rags was doing in the middle of the road and went over to have a look. As soon as the priest saw that the heap was actually a man lying bleeding in the dust, he quickly crossed to the other side of the road. He didn't want to know what had happened or have anything to do with it."

The lawyer gasped, "How could such a holy man not help someone in need?"

"The next traveller to approach was a Levite," Jesus carried on.

"This man is sure to help," said the Lawyer. Jews from the tribe of Levi were so god-fearing that priests were always chosen from among them.

"The Levite shuddered in disgust when he saw the battered and bruised man barely alive," Jesus continued. "Like the 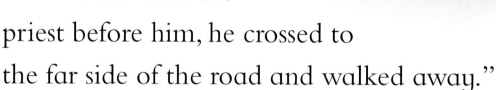 priest before him, he crossed to the far side of the road and walked away."

Now the lawyer was really shocked. A holy Levite should have known better.

"Next, a Samaritan passed by," Jesus announced.

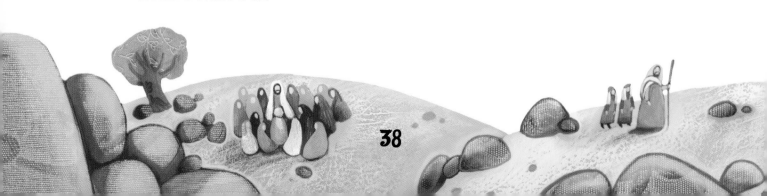

The lawyer pulled a face. Samaritans were the people who had been sent to live in Israel when the Jews were taken away as slaves by the Babylonians. The Jews hated the Samaritans for taking their land. They also looked down on the Samaritans because they weren't God's Chosen People and often didn't worship God at all. The lawyer thought the Samaritan probably went over to see if there was anything left to steal!

But Jesus continued, "The Samaritan was appalled when he saw the dying man and rushed to help. He gave the poor man some water, heaved him up onto his donkey and hurried to the nearest town. There he paid an innkeeper to take him in and look after him until he was better."

The lawyer was flabbergasted.

"Now which of the three travellers would you say was the neighbour of the attacked man?" Jesus asked.

"The one who helped him," stuttered the lawyer.

"Right," said Jesus. "Now go and behave like the Samaritan."

Luke chapter 10

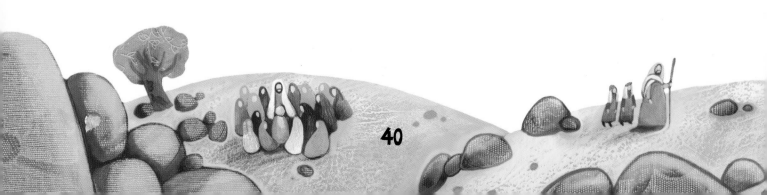